THE
JOLLY POSTMAN

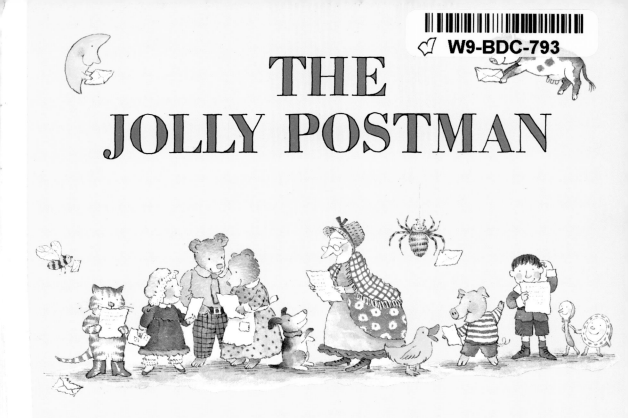

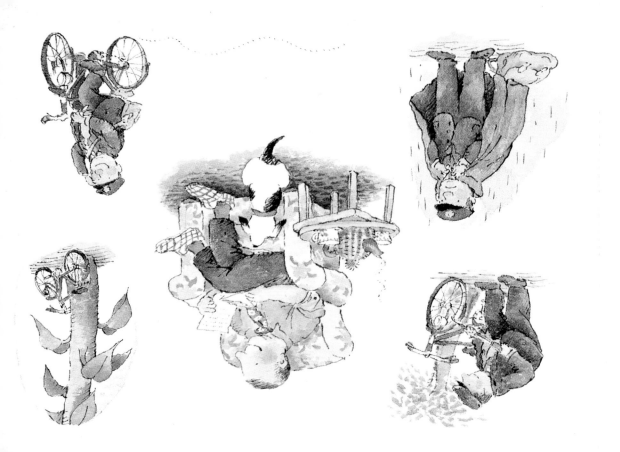

Off went the Postman, Toodle-oo!

Off went the Postman,
Toodle-oo!

Now the Jolly Postman,
   Nearly done (so is the story),
Came to a house where a party had begun.

Now the Jolly Postman,
    Nearly done (so is the story),
Came to a house where a party had begun.

So 'Grandma' read the letter
And poured the tea

So 'Grandma' read the letter
And poured the tea

Later on, the Postman,
Feeling hot,
Came upon a 'grandma' in a shady spot.

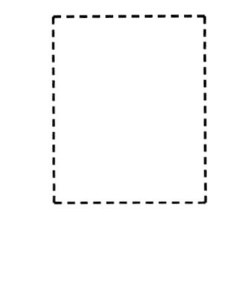

Later on, the Postman,
Feeling hot,
Came upon a 'grandma' in a shady spot.

CINDERELLA

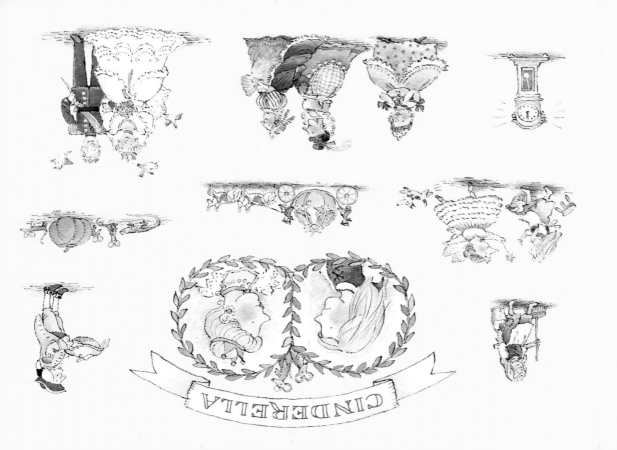

CINDERELLA

So the Giant read the postcard
With Baby on his knee

So the Giant read the postcard
With Baby on his knee

- -

- -

- -

- -

- -

PAR AVION
VIA AIR MAIL

EAST OF SUN
3:15 PM
18 MAY
1986
WEST OF MOON

1 50

MR V. BIGG
MILE HIGH HOUSE
BEANSTALK GARDENS

MR V. BIGG
MILE HIGH HOUSE
BEANSTALK GARDENS

PAR AVION
VIA AIR MAIL

EAST OF SUN
3.15PM
18 MAY
1986
WEST OF MOON

150

So the Witch read the letter
With a cackle of glee

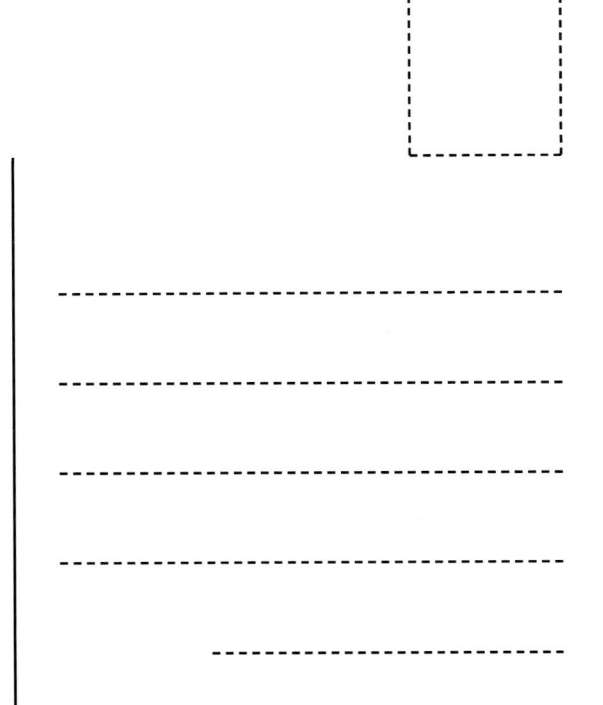

So the Witch read the letter
With a cackle of glee

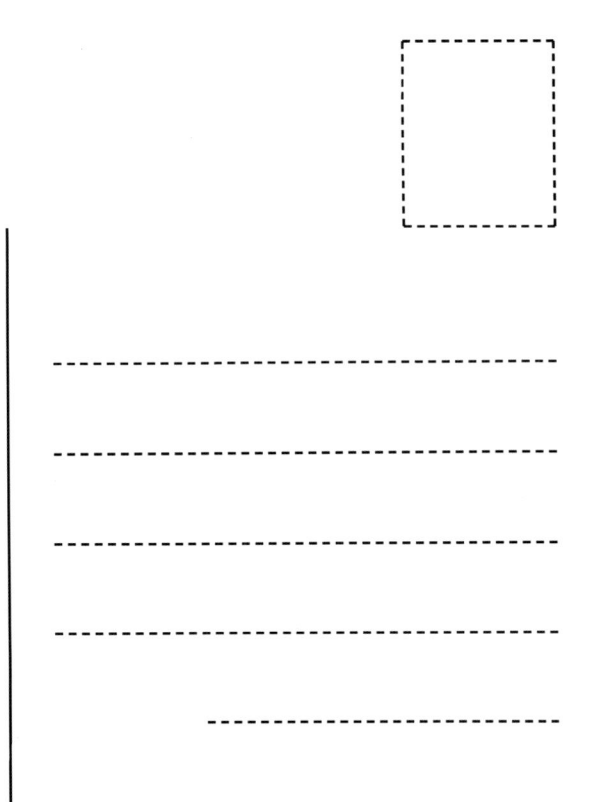

HOBGOBLIN SUPPLIES LTD©

Everything for the modern witch.
Delivered to your door or den.
Covens catered for.

Cup and SORCERER
tea service
*it washes
itself!*

SKY HIGH
goggles
Fits all sizes

— Wheeeee!

the perfect pick-me-up

Witching Hour
Glass ~
*The ideal
gift*

REJUVENATING PILLS

Witcho

Feeling low? Take WITCHO

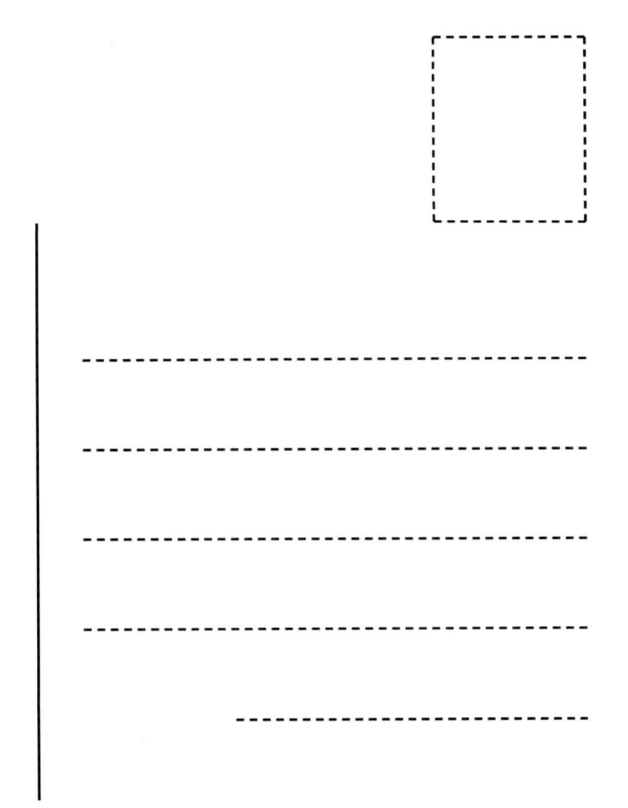

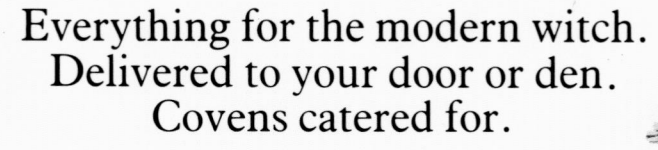

HOBGOBLIN SUPPLIES LTD©

Everything for the modern witch.
Delivered to your door or den.
Covens catered for.

Cup and SORCERER
tea service
*it washes
itself!*

SKY HIGH
goggles
Fits all sizes

— Wheeeee!

Witching Hour
Glass ~
*The ideal
gift*

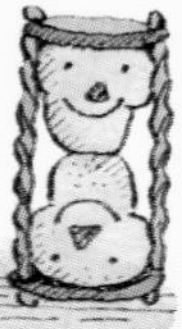

REJUVENATING PILLS

Witcho

the perfect pick-me-up

Feeling low? Take WITCHO

Once upon a bicycle,
  So they say,
A Jolly Postman came one day

Once upon a bicycle,
  So they say,
A Jolly Postman came one day

Mr and Mrs Bear
<u>Three</u> Bears Cottage
<u>The</u> Woods

Mr and Mrs Bear
<u>Three</u> Bears Cottage
<u>The</u> Woods

18p

BANBURY CROSS
4 15PM
20 MAY
1986
K81